CU00409126

THE
FUNNIEST
UNITED
QUOTES...
EVER!

By Gordon Law

Also available to buy

Printed in the United States of America
ISBN-13: 978-1539778318
ISBN-10: 1539778312

Photos courtesy of: Twocoms/Shutterstock.com and Michael Hulf.

Contents

Introduction

When Sir Alex Ferguson described the pressure of the title run-in back in 2003 as "squeaky-bum time" it wasn't long before it became common football parlance.

That was one of many brilliant one-liners from the Manchester United manager during his glorious reign that will forever be remembered.

Whether it was 'knocking Liverpool off their perch', dismissing noisy neighbours, his comic musings on players or unleashing the famous hairdryer, Ferguson was a quote machine.

His long-running war of words with Arsenal counterpart Arsene Wenger as the two clubs battled for Premier League supremacy was enthralling. And we also had Ferguson's battle with referees and the famous 'Fergie time'.

The former boss wasn't the only Red Devil that has kept the football world entertained and many United players should have just let their feet do the talking instead of their mouths.

David Beckham was prone to the most ridiculous comments and there were the bizarre statements from football philosopher and poet Eric Cantona.

We've had George Best's tales of off-field antics and Cristiano Ronaldo's strange obsession with himself, while Rio Ferdinand and Wayne Rooney have put out some truly embarrassing tweets.

With the immensely quotable Zlatan Ibrahimovic and Jose Mourinho at Old Trafford, we can expect even more hilarious moments. So tuck into this unique collection of United zingers. Enjoy!

Gordon Law

THE FUNNIEST UNITED QUOTES... EVER!

TALKING BALLS

"If he was an inch taller he'd be the best centre half in Britain. His father is 6ft 2in – I'd check the milkman."

Sir Alex Ferguson on Gary Neville

"[Ole Gunnar] Solskjaer never misses the target. That time he hit the post."

Peter Schmeichel

"Bobby Collins was so small, we used to say he was the only player in the league who had turn-ups on his shorts."

George Best

"I never understood a word Alex Ferguson was saying. One day I walked into the dressing room and he was staring at me. He motioned at me to cut my hair, so I did later that day. In training the next day, he didn't recognise me. I went past him several times and he didn't have a clue who I was."

Bebe

"Peter Schmeichel once asked for a shoe horn. Schmikes keeps you on your toes every match. It can take 20 minutes just to set out his stuff. He doesn't always require the shoe horn, but I keep it handy just in case."

Former United kitman Norman Davies

"For the players he left behind at Manchester United, there will be one lasting memory of Gary Birtles. His weird, way-out gear... the fancy bow ties, winged collars and spectacular suits that no one else would wear without the courage of four bottles of wine."

Steve Coppell

"Becks hasn't changed since I've known him. He's always been a flash Cockney git."

Ryan Giggs

"Rio thinks he's Snoop the dog."

Pat Crerand on Rio Ferdinand after he rapped at United's title-winning parade

"When he [Alex Ferguson] starts with the hairdryer treatment on them, I've seen foreign players turn pink and black players turn white."

Rio Ferdinand

"Peter [Schmeichel] returns but the operation has not worked because he still won't admit it when he has made a mistake."

Brian McClair

"You couldn't turn off the floodlights until Nobby [Stiles] had gone home because he needed to find his contact lenses after the game."

Sir Bobby Charlton

"I don't know where Carlos keeps the dummy. He produces it from nowhere."

Michael Carrick on Carlos Tevez's unique goal celebration

"He [David Beckham] cannot kick with his left foot, he cannot head a ball, he cannot tackle and he doesn't score many goals. Apart from that he's all right."

George Best

"There's no way Ryan Giggs is another George Best. He's another Ryan Giggs."

Denis Law

"You can never beat Alex Ferguson and when you do, you come off second best."

Steve McClaren

"Paul Ince wants everyone to call him Guv'nor, but we call him Incey."

Lee Sharpe

"I'm going to see what he's been eating and copy everything he's doing. He must have been very lucky with his genetics."

Rio Ferdinand on Ryan Giggs, aged 40

"I told Eric he couldn't go to court wearing a shirt unbuttoned to the chest. He said, 'I am Cantona. I can go as I want'. He got 14 days in prison and I thought, Oh my God, it must be the shirt."

Paul Ince

"Matt [Busby] was the eternal optimist. In 1968, he still hoped that Glenn Miller was just missing."

Pat Crerand

"Get up. Go to work. Play the game. Get showered. Go home."

Paul Scholes

United chairman Louis Edwards: "We've received more than 30 applications for the post of Manchester United manager."

Wilf McGuinness: "Yes and I wrote all of them."

McGuinness is unveiled as the new boss at a United press conference in 1969

"David Beckham will not be asked to take a turn in the black chair on Mastermind."

Jaap Stam

"He was able to use either foot. Sometimes he seemed to have six."

Sir Matt Busby on George Best

"I don't understand Mr Ferguson when he is speaking normally, so when he yells it's even more difficult."

Mikael Silvestre

"Ryan just put his head down, ran like he always does, didn't pass and got lucky."

Nicky Butt on Ryan Giggs' great goal in the 1999 FA Cup semi-final against Arsenal

"The only thing I have in common with George Best is that we come from the same place, played for the same club and were discovered by the same man."

Norman Whiteside

"I do have a celebration planned – I'm going to strip naked and run round the stadium!"

Anderson reveals his plan if he scores in the Champions League final

"Well, I rose like a salmon at the far post, but Pally rose like a fresher salmon above me, headed the ball at the keeper, the keeper fumbled, then I saw a sudden flash of brilliant red and leathered it into the roof of the net with my left foot sponsored by Diadora."

David May remembers his goal in United's 4-0 win against Porto in superb detail

"We always looked forward to playing Aston Villa to hear him mangle Ugo Ehiogu's name. 'Make sure you pick up Ehugu, Ehogy, whatever his name is'."

Gary Neville on Sir Alex Ferguson

"Peter Schmeichel reckons the present Man United side [in 1999] would beat the 1968 European Cup winners. He's got a point, because we're all over 50 now."

Nobby Stiles

"Paul Scholes – the most complete mental player I've ever seen."

Ex-United youth player Ben Thornley

"There was no point in him coming to team talks. All I used to say was, 'Whenever possible, pass the ball to George'."

Sir Matt Busby on George Best

"That's my philosophy, the players have to accept the captain. The first captain is Wayne Rooney, the second captain is Michael Carrick, and last year the third captain was Mr Mike Smalling. Sorry, I mean Chris Smalling."

Louis van Gaal

"Goalscorer, winner and funny."

United manager Jose Mourinho describes Zlatan Ibrahimovic in three words

"Gary Neville was having a piss one day, 45 yards away by a fence. Scholes whacked him right in the arse."

Sir Alex Ferguson on Paul Scholes' shooting accuracy

"Bring an umbrella! And yesterday I couldn't believe that it was raining in the training ground, so it was great advice. The second advice was to bring my typical bottle of wine because now we are going to have many occasions to be together."

United boss Jose Mourinho reveals Sir Alex Ferguson gave him some important advice

"We named Sir Alex 'The Hairdryer' because he would come right up to your face and scream at you."

Gary Pallister

"When I scored my first goal for England, I was so excited I didn't know what to do or where to run. David [Beckham] just pointed and said, 'The England fans are that way, mate'."

Wayne Rooney

"Nobby Stiles a dirty player? No, he's never hurt anyone. Mind you, he's frightened a few."

Sir Matt Busby

"People look at me and Keane and look back to our Manchester United days and think we are snarling, horrible people. But we are not like that. We are nice guys, family men."

Paul Ince

"I remember my shock and awe seeing Dion Dublin coming out of the shower. I mean, it was just magnificent."

Sir Alex Ferguson on Dion Dublin's manhood

"Norman Whiteside was more a scorer of great goals than a great scorer of goals."

Paul McGrath

"The man knows everything about you, what your parents' names are, your sister's name, your brother's name."

Phil Neville on Sir Alex Ferguson

"I sent my son to one of his schools of excellence and he came back bald."

George Best on Sir Bobby Charlton

"Wayne [Rooney] is only 17 but Sachin Tendulkar didn't become an Indian cricket legend by him being kept back because of his age."

Gary Neville

"The gaffer said at the end of his team talk,

'Has anybody got any questions?' 'Yes', I said.

'Where do babies come from?'"

Brian McClair

"Here at Old Trafford, they reckon Bestie had

double-jointed ankles."

Sir Alex Ferguson on George Best

UNITED VS THE WORLD

"I think he was an angry man. He must have been disturbed for some reason. I think you have got to cut through the venom of it and hopefully he'll reflect and understand what he said was absolutely ridiculous."

Sir Alex Ferguson on Rafa Benitez's memorable 'fact' rant in 2009

"They got away with murder. What the Arsenal players did was the worst I have witnessed in sport."

Sir Alex Ferguson the Battle of Old Trafford in 2003

"For me, Liverpool is a fantastic club. Because I have won every game against Liverpool."
Louis van Gaal enjoys his 100 per cent winning record over the Reds

"I went over to take a kick where the Chelsea fans were and they started chucking sticks of celery and sweetcorn. It made me laugh to think of them popping into the greengrocers' shops on the way to Wembley."
Ryan Giggs on the 1994 FA Cup final

"I can't stand Liverpool, I can't stand the people, I can't stand anything to do with them."
Gary Neville on Liverpool

"It's City isn't it? They are a small club with a small mentality. All they can talk about is Manchester United. They can't get away from it. They think taking Tevez away from Manchester United is a triumph. It is poor stuff."

Sir Alex Ferguson on that Carlos Tevez poster

"I'm made from a little bit of iron. So I have a shield, an iron shield. Everybody can write or speak about me and I cannot change that."

Louis van Gaal says he can handle himself after Chelsea manager Jose Mourinho's attempts at mind games

"We're now the most successful team in English football. And obviously being an Evertonian, it is all the more special for me that it is United's 19th title – and the one that has taken us past our main rivals Liverpool."

Wayne Rooney

"Sometimes you have a noisy neighbour. You cannot do anything about that. They will always be noisy. You just have to get on with your life, put your television on and turn it up a bit louder."

Sir Alex Ferguson on their Manchester rivals

"Our programme didn't do us any favours and I think we have been handicapped by the Premier League in the fixture list. They tell me it's not planned. Bloody hell!"

Sir Alex Ferguson

"Do they hate us? You go to take a corner at Elland Road and you've got 15,000 horrible skinheads in their end yelling murder at you."

Ryan Giggs on Leeds fans

"I expect abuse, but I also got a hamburger and about £4.50 in change."

Gary Neville on items thrown at him by Liverpool fans

30

"I read that Scolari is more experienced than me. What have I been doing for the last 34 years? I must have missed something or been asleep somewhere. They are saying because of Scolari's experience, Chelsea are going to win the league. I don't understand that."

Sir Alex Ferguson on new Chelsea manager 'Big' Phil Scolari

"A scouser knocks Liverpool of there perch. Haha. An evertoniian aswell. Yes. People. U can't imagine how happy I am tonight. Believe"

Wayne Rooney tweets after United's title triumph in May 2011

"I grew up an Everton fan, my whole family are Everton fans and I grew up hating Liverpool. And that hasn't changed."

Wayne Rooney

"My greatest challenge is not what's happening at the moment, my greatest challenge was knocking Liverpool right off their f*cking perch. And you can print that."

Sir Alex Ferguson

"When I was younger I used to get abuse off the Leeds fans, who sang things like, 'There's only one spotty virgin'."

Ryan Giggs

"Clubs come away from Anfield choking on their own vomit and biting their own tongues knowing they have been done by the referee."

Sir Alex Ferguson on Colin Gibson's red card at Anfield in a 3-3 draw in 1988

"I think I've always shown the right respect to Liverpool and the history they have and great team they are. But I also know that it's the team I get the most pleasure out of beating."

Ryan Giggs

"I don't get a great reception at Anfield I must say – I'm not their favourite son!"

Gary Neville on Liverpool

"Don't swap shirts with those dirty b*stards."

Sir Alex Ferguson on Champions League opponents Feyenoord

WOMAN TROUBLE

"My wife picked me out of a football sticker album and I chose her from a music video off the television."

David Beckham

"I don't really like the attention from girls – apart from anything else I already have a girlfriend. I like supporters of football whatever sex they are, but it's not so great when you're on a night out and girls just sit next to you... but to be honest it doesn't happen to me that often anyway."

Gary Neville

"The truth is some women will do anything to crack on with footballers. Some birds will buy you drinks all night, strip for you, get shagged with other people in the room, and do all sorts of tricks."

Rio Ferdinand

"My wife cringes every time someone calls me 'Sir Alex' or calls her 'Lady Cathy'. She says, 'I don't know why you accepted it in the first place'."

Sir Alex Ferguson

"Gazza said that scoring was better than an orgasm. Lee Chapman reckoned it wasn't as good. I'll go with Pele – he thought it was about the same."

Ryan Giggs

"I used to go missing a lot... Miss Canada, Miss United Kingdom, Miss World."

George Best

"I dated a girl from Manchester and she showed me that steak pies and chips are very good."

Cristiano Ronaldo

"That wife of mine just bullies me. She throws me out of the door at seven o'clock every morning! So that's a definite no. Oh no, I dare not risk the wrath of that lass from the Gorbals."

Sir Alex Ferguson claims that it's his wife Cathy who stops him from retiring

"Choosing between City and Liverpool to take the title is like choosing which bloke nicks your wife."

Gary Neville

"The word 'desire' is fantastic. We need desire, hunger and a lot of times I use the word 'horny' to my players."

Louis van Gaal ahead of United's Europa League tie with Midtjylland

"Being part of #mufc history is something I am proud of! Special shout to the dinner ladies!"

Rio Ferdinand's tweet

"Liz Hurley, she's nice. I'd take her to Pizza Express – no posh restaurants. We'd go for a pizza then to watch Grease or something."

Phil Neville on his perfect date

"Beckham thought that a celebrity lifestyle, being drawn increasingly into the showbiz world of wife Victoria, was compatible with the regime of a professional footballer. His manager did not."

Sir Bobby Charlton

"I told her I had a match but she wasn't having any of it. She said it was a friendly and that I had to help her to pack because we're moving house."

Sir Alex Ferguson on wife Cathy

"When I was an apprentice there was this lad who really fancied himself with the girls. We were on this tour in Ireland and he went up to this girl, gave her 10 pence and said, 'Ring your mum, tell her you're not coming home tonight'. And it worked actually! But I've never used it myself."

Ryan Giggs

"Will I ever play in Italy? Never say never in life. I do gladly travel there, like I did last summer, because there are the most beautiful and sexiest girls in the world."

Cristiano Ronaldo

"When you see what Huth is doing to Fellaini, that's a penalty. "Shall I grab you by your hair? What is your reaction when I grab your hair? (he grabs reporter's hair). Your hair is shorter than Fellaini but when I do that, what are you doing then? It's a reaction. Every human being who is grabbed by the hair, only with sex masochism, then it is allowed but not in other situations. They did it. They did it several times I think."

Louis van Gaal defends Marouane Fellaini after his alleged elbow on Leicester's Robert Huth

"I've been punished for falling in love. What I have done has nothing at all to do with my track record as a manager."

Tommy Docherty after being fired by United in 1977 when his relationship with the physio's wife was made public

"Me and Wilf McGuinness both got the sack from Manchester United, but to this day I don't know whose wife Wilf was seeing."

Tommy Docherty

"He was never a problem until he got married."

Sir Alex Ferguson on David Beckham

"Could I not have two bullets?"

Sir Alex Ferguson when asked if he had a bullet in a gun, would he use it on Arsene Wenger or Victoria Beckham

"I always used to go for blondes and quiet girls, but Victoria is the total opposite – dark and loud."

David Beckham

"The ball is like a woman, she loves to be caressed."

Eric Cantona

I was with David the fateful night he first saw the Spice Girls on telly and said, 'See that girl who can't dance or sing? I'm going to marry her'."

Gary Neville on how David Beckham fell for Victoria

MEDIA CIRCUS

"Has anybody in this room not a feeling to apologise to me? That's what I am wondering. I think I was already sacked, I have read. Or have been sacked."

Louis van Gaal blasts journalists at a pre-match press conference

"You f*cking sell your papers and radio shows off the back of this club."

Sir Alex Ferguson

"Half an hour? You could shoot Ben Hur in half an hour. You've got 15 seconds."

Ron Atkinson to a photographer who asked him for 30 minutes of his time

"We don't speak about Wayne Rooney, you have criticised him. I don't – you! [pointing at a reporter] You too, fat man!"

Louis van Gaal gets personal with a journalist as he was on his way out of a media conference

Reporter: "Do you remember where you were when United won the treble in '99?"

Denis Irwin: "Oh yes. I was playing left back."

"Do you fancy me or something?"

David Beckham after a male journalist asked about his latest haircut

Ron Saunders: "Giving the press boys the usual old rubbish, Ron?"

Ron Atkinson: "Yes, Ron. I was just telling them what a good manager you are."

"You've enthralled me all season with your honesty, integrity – and nonsense!"

Sir Alex Ferguson. One journalist retorted: "Likewise!"

"I cannot change that. I cannot change facts and you know that."

An under-pressure Louis van Gaal on being asked about Radamel Falcao's lack of goals

"Gotta say if Sky Sports News went pay per view on the last day of transfer window I'd pay and get my popcorn + ice cream out all day!"

Rio Ferdinand tweets

"I try to be honest. Some of you don't write it the way I say it."

David Moyes

"I am allowed to toast with you, my friends of the media. Merry Christmas. I wish your family a lot of love, health and happiness. Cheers. Not a bad wine. (It is) our sponsor."

Louis van Gaal ironically hands out some ironic seasons greetings

Journalist: "What's the John Gidman situation, Ron? Is he in plaster?"
Ron Atkinson: "No, he's in Marbella."

"We played the best match of the season. You don't think so? It's good that you want to know what I think."
Louis van Gaal to a reporter after a draw with Chelsea

"You're welcome to my phone number, gentlemen, but please remember not to ring me during The Sweeney."
Ron Atkinson on his first day as United manager

"I don't give any of you credibility. You talk about wanting to have an association with people here and you wonder why I don't get on with you? But you're a f*cking embarrassment. One of these days the door is going to be shut on you permanently."

Sir Alex Ferguson fires shots at the press

Presenter: "You dropped your head when Pele announced your name. Was that a relief?"

Cristiano Ronaldo: "No, I was just checking my flies."

The winger speaking after the 2009 FIFA Player of the Year awards

Journalist: "What's the strangest aspect of English culture you've noticed?"

Nemanja Vidic: "Driving on the left and tea with milk."

"I'm here to discuss Manchester United, not one player. You want a headline, I want a team performance."

Sir Alex Ferguson

A FUNNY OLD GAME

"Balloon ball. The percentage game. Route one. It has crept into the First Division. We get asked to loan youngsters to these teams. We don't do it. They come back with bad habits, big legs and good eyesight."
Ron Atkinson

"The most important difference is that I am training the players, not in the legs, but in the brain, in brain power."
Louis van Gaal's footballing philosophy

"We are happy with three points, but it could have been more."
Ryan Giggs

"I'm pleased to have avoided the English teams at this stage. Emotionally and physically it would have been draining – probably more than against a European team."

Rio Ferdinand forgets that England is in fact in Europe

"I'm not at Manchester United to keep everyone happy."

Roy Keane makes his point

"It's the best day since I got married."

Sir Alex Ferguson after a win at Sheffield United in 1992

"This team never lose games – they just run out of time occasionally."

United coach Steve McClaren

"People used to say that if I'd shot John Lennon, he'd still be alive today."

Gary Birtles on a lean scoring run at United

"People are looking for reasons why we are not doing well but it is only because we have not been playing well."

David Moyes

"I used to dream about taking the ball round the keeper, stopping it on the line and then getting down on my hands and knees and heading it into the net."

George Best

"When I looked down, the leg was lying one way and my ankle was pointing towards Hong Kong – so I knew I was in serious trouble."

Alan Smith

"It wasn't my choice to become a goalkeeper, but I was probably too violent to play outfield."

Peter Schmeichel

"After I scored six against Northampton I hung back for the last part of the game. I didn't want to score any more. It was getting embarrassing."

George Best

"It was one of those goals that's invariably a goal."

Denis Law

"Football. Bloody hell."

Sir Alex Ferguson after United had beaten Bayern to win the Champions League

"No one will ever equal Sir Matt Busby's achievements and influence at Old Trafford, but I'd like to go down as someone who nearly did as much."

Tommy Docherty

"Well, I can play in the centre, on the right and occasionally on the left side."

David Beckham when asked if he was a "volatile player"

"When they first installed all-seater stadiums, everyone predicted that the fans wouldn't stand for it."

George Best

"It's getting tickly now – squeaky-bum time, I call it. It's going to be an interesting few weeks and the standard of the Premiership is such that nothing will be easy."

Sir Alex Ferguson's now world famous expression to describe the pressure of the title run-in back in 2003

"If we played like that every week, we wouldn't be so inconsistent."

Bryan Robson

"You shouldn't be nuts, but it doesn't matter if you are a bit peculiar."

Peter Schmeichel

"Away from home our fans are fantastic, I'd call them the hardcore fans. But at home they have a few drinks and probably the prawn sandwiches, and they don't realise what's going on out on the pitch. I don't think some of the people who come to Old Trafford can spell 'football', never mind understand it."

Roy Keane on the prawn-sandwich brigade

"When I came to Manchester from the North East aged 15, I didn't know what a director was or what he did. My dad would have explained it as someone who didn't work."

Bobby Charlton on becoming a United director

"I have said to you that you are the best fans of the world but I was tonight a little bit disappointed. And I shall say why. I have seen a lady who plays the saxophone fantastically. Give her a big applause!"

Louis van Gaal at United's 2014/15 end-of-season season awards

"I had to get rid of this idea that Manchester United were a drinking club, rather than a football club."

Sir Alex Ferguson referring to issues with Norman Whiteside and Paul McGrath

"Being a robot, devoid of passion and spirit, is obviously the way forward for the modern-day footballer."

Gary Neville

"Many times I went out to hurt a player because that was my job."

Roy Keane

"We gave away two terrible goals but prior to that we passed the ball brilliantly, kept the ball and had great control of the game."

David Moyes after a 2-0 defeat against Everton – his last match as manager

"Some people tell me that we professional players are soccer slaves. Well, if this is slavery, give me a life sentence."

Bobby Charlton talking about the maximum wage in 1960

"Before the game there was all this stuff about anti-racism and anti-bullying. It would be a good idea to start wearing wristbands for anti-diving."

Roy Keane

"It was a draw so in the end we didn't win."

David Beckham

"It's interesting that the games in which we've dropped points are those where we've failed to score."

Sir Alex Ferguson

"It was a sense of numbness really – how the hell are we out of this World Cup? It even got to the point where there were weird ideas – maybe if we'd had brown rice rather than white."

Rio Ferdinand on England's 2006 exit

"We've ended the season on a high – apart from the last game, which we lost."

David Beckham

"Everyone says the power is with the players, but that is just not true. As a player, you are nothing more than a piece of meat. We're nothing more than cattle."

Jaap Stam is not happy with his treatment at United and claimed Roy Keane agreed, saying: "Jaap, they sold you like a cow."

"It was particularly pleasing that our goalscorers scored tonight."

Sir Alex Ferguson

"Great managers have to be ugly and swear a lot."

George Best

"We have won more games with 4-4-2, but when you analyse the games, we have twitched our ass. I said to my players I was squeezing my ass, but it was the wrong expression. I have twitched my ass on the bench because we were out of balance."

Louis van Gaal

"If it's not a contract I want then I won't sign it. That's not a threat."

Roy Keane

"Being at United was a culture shock for me. Even the loos had gold taps."

Gary Birtles

"I don't like losing but I've mellowed. I maybe have a short fuse but it goes away quicker now."

Sir Alex Ferguson

"We didn't play badly. We deserved to win, if not win, at worst draw."

David Moyes after losing to Spurs

BEST OF ENEMIES

"My problem with Paul McGrath was whether to give him appearance money or disappearance money."

Ron Atkinson

"Maybe Gary deserves to be chased up a tunnel every now and then – there would be a queue for him, probably. But you have to draw a line eventually."

Roy Keane on Gary Neville's popularity

"A great manager, but not, in my opinion, a great man."

Tommy Docherty on Sir Alex Ferguson

"It seems Ferguson is the president of England. Each time he speaks badly about a player, and he has said the worst about me, I never asked him to apologise. But if somebody makes a joke about him, you must apologise to him. But I don't apologise. There's no relationship at all between me and Ferguson."

Carlos Tevez

"I would rather sit down and have a cuppa with Neil Ruddock, who broke my leg in two places in 1996, than with Teddy Sheringham, who I've pretty much detested for the past 15 years."

Andy Cole

"Who do you think you are having meetings about me? You were a crap player and you are a crap manager. The only reason I have any dealings with you is that somehow you are the manager of my country and you're not even Irish, you English c*nt!"

Roy Keane on Republic of Ireland manager Mick McCarthy

"I moved to Manchester and stayed at [agent Paul] Stretford's house. He made me part of the family. I thought it was a generous gesture. I later found out he'd been deducting rent from my earnings."

Andy Cole

"Half a million for Remi Moses? You could get the original Moses for that and the tablets as well."

Tommy Docherty

"When I signed Jim Holton from Shrewsbury for £100,000, Harry Gregg told me I had a player who didn't know the meaning of the word defeat. I told him defeat wasn't the only word he didn't understand. There was also pass, control, dribble..."

Tommy Docherty

"Eric Cantona couldn't tackle a fish supper."

Sir Alex Ferguson

"You have an expression in England and it is, 'Sticks and stones can break my bones, but names can never hurt me'. It is a fantastic expression. Why is he saying something? The benefit of the club, or the benefit of himself?"

Louis van Gaal after Paul Scholes criticised United's style of football

"There is a shortage of characters in this team. It seems to be in this club that you have to play badly to be rewarded. Maybe that is what I should do when I come back. Play badly."

Roy Keane blasts his teammates

"The last time I won a title was one year ago. It wasn't ten years ago, 15 years ago. One year ago. So if I have a lot to prove, imagine the others."

Jose Mourinho takes a swipe at Arsene Wenger in his first United press conference

"I could approach this job in a defensive point of view by saying, 'The last three years the best we did was fourth and an FA Cup'."

The new United boss has another dig

"If that lad makes a First Division footballer, my name is Mao Tse-tung."

Tommy Docherty on Dwight Yorke

"He can't run, can't tackle and can't head a ball. The only time he goes forward is to toss the coin."

Tommy Docherty on Ray Wilkins

"Roy Keane is Damien, the devil incarnate off the film The Omen. He's evil. Even in training."

Ryan Giggs

"I'll f*cking see you out there!"

Roy Keane to Arsenal's Patrick Vieira in the tunnel

Best of Enemies

"Just because you are paid £120,000 a week and play well for 20 minutes against Tottenham, you think you are a superstar."

Roy Keane on Rio Ferdinand

"When you do bad things, he still wants to kill you, but that is a good thing for a manager."

Cristiano Ronaldo on Sir Alex Ferguson

"@piersmorgan shut up u egg and get out of cowells hole. Won't tell u again."

Wayne Rooney tweets he is not a fan of Piers Morgan on Britain's Got Talent

"Wayne Rooney always struck me as a very angry young man, always arguing with people outside the training ground, especially on the phone. He seemed to fly into a rage about the smallest things and went through mobile phones like they were sweets. He'd smash phones up in frustration, throwing them on the concrete."

Rio Ferdinand

"I'd waited long enough. I f*cking hit him hard. The ball was there (I think). Take that you c*nt. And don't ever stand over me sneering about fake injuries."

Roy Keane on his Alf Inge Haaland tackle

"I could see Fergie's face turning purple. 'Club car?' he yelled. 'You've got more chance of getting a club bike'."

Ryan Giggs

"If Tommy Docherty says, 'Good morning' to you, check the weather."

George Best

"You're a f*cking bottler Incey! You cannae handle the stage, can you? You are a f*cking bottler!"

Sir Alex Ferguson to Paul Ince at half-time in a Champions League tie

"[Patrick] Vieira was bragging about all the things he'd done in Senegal. I said to him, 'If you're so f*cking worried about Senegal, why didn't you play for them?'"

Roy Keane

"Roy Keane has no manners. There's never any reason not to be polite, even with people you don't like."

George Best

LIFESTYLE CHOICE

"A chap was once trying to get me to play for his club in America. 'We'll pay you $20,000 this year and $30,000 next year'. OK, I replied. I'll sign next year."

George Best

"Some players are cocky gits. You see them out and about, giving it large but they haven't done anything in the game to justify it."

Roy Keane

"Before every game I usually go to Burger King or McDonald's – very good for the hamstring."

Patrice Evra

"The manager doesn't want me to live like a monk. If he tried to make me live like a monk my football would go down the drain. He understands that, we've had that conversation."

Dwight Yorke

"Our lives are quite boring. I spend a lot of time watching Coronation Street and EastEnders."

Rio Ferdinand

"When we went paintballing, it got into a bit of a free-for-all. It hurts when you get hit and there's a few sadistic people in our squad – David May springs to mind."

Gary Neville

"I have not got accustomed to English life. The food is truly disastrous and it rains all the time."

Patrice Evra is enjoying it in Manchester

"I not only like to have the TV and light on to help me sleep, but also a vacuum cleaner. Failing that, a fan or hairdryer will do. I've ruined so many hairdryers by letting them burn out. So far I haven't set fire to anywhere."

Wayne Rooney

"People always say I shouldn't be burning the candle at both ends. Maybe they haven't got a big enough candle."

George Best

"I'm a little embarrassed to be named a chief.
I'm not sure I'm worthy. It's something to tell
the lads – I'm sure they'll be very happy to call
me chief!"

**Rio Ferdinand after being given the title
'Chief Fiwagboola' by Nigeria's King Akiolu
when he helped launch a children's football
programme**

"I never socialised with Eric. My wife and I
always said we'd have him over, but we never
got round to it. We always called round for the
rent, but never to ask him over. That's terrible
really, isn't it?"

**Mark Hughes on being Eric Cantona's
landlord**

"Sometimes you go into Nando's and you want to tuck into the chicken wings with your fingers but you know someone's watching you, so you don't. I'm thinking, 'If these chicken wings were at home they would get demolished'. But I have to use a knife and fork. You end up saying, 'Could I get a bag to take these home, please'."

Danny Welbeck

"I listen to 50 Cent, Jay-Z, Stereophonics, Arctic Monkeys, also the musical Oliver – I can sing every tune."

Wayne Rooney

"I don't know why people are so interested in what I wear on holiday... this year it was the pink hat with the flower – I don't see what is wrong with it."

Cristiano Ronaldo loves the attention

"There is no winter break and I think that is the most evil thing of this culture. I have a wife, kids and grandchildren, and I cannot see them at Christmas."

Louis van Gaal is unhappy with the festive programme

"I'd give all the champagne I've ever drunk to have played with Eric Cantona on a big European night at Old Trafford."

George Best

"In 1969 I gave up women and alcohol. It was the worst 20 minutes of my life."

George Best

"I have come to accept that if I have a new haircut it is front page news. But having a picture of my foot on the front page of a national newspaper is a bit exceptional."

David Beckham on the coverage of his metatarsal injury

Lifestyle Choice

"Let me recommend shopping to any young professional football player who feels they're in danger of going off the rails. It has less risk of personal injury than a punch-up outside a nightclub and you very rarely end up with a hangover."

Brian McClair

"The players go on to the training pitch clutching cups of coffee. Apparently they are given bacon sandwiches with all kinds of colourful sauces. That would be unthinkable in France."

Mikael Silvestre

"If you'd given me the choice of going out and beating four men and smashing a goal in from 30 yards against Liverpool or going to bed with Miss World, it would have been a difficult choice. Luckily, I had both."

George Best

"A lot of people tell me that I look like [actor] Andy Garcia. He has actually influenced my choice of hairstyle and I have even studied the way he smokes so I can hold my cigarette in the same way."

Dimitar Berbatov

"My wife is at home after returning from the Netherlands and the wine is already open. It is probably the most expensive bottle of wine because I have received that from Ed Woodward. I always get expensive wine when we beat an opponent from the top six and we beat Liverpool. I don't get any wine tonight for beating Derby, I only get it when I beat a club out of the top six in the Premier League!"

Louis van Gaal

"Just to confirm to all my followers I have had a hair transplant. I was going bald at 25, why not."

Wayne Rooney tweets

"I don't normally cook, but if I did it probably would be beans, sausage, bacon and eggs. I never really get to eat that to be honest."

Wayne Rooney

"I spent a lot of money on booze, women and fast cars. The rest I just squandered."

George Best

"Life's tough. I've had to swap my Merc for a BMW, I'm down to my last 37 suits and I'm drinking non-vintage champagne."

Ron Atkinson after being fired by United

Lifestyle Choice

"There is no chance I would ever consider having all my hair cut off. My hair is my life. It's so important to me. If you cut off my hair, it is like cutting out my heart or cutting off my legs. I would cry for days and days."

Anderson

"Of course I miss Manchester; it felt I left a family back there. I especially miss the apple crumble and custard they served at Carrington after training."

Cristiano Ronaldo

"When I see a group of men walking towards me, it's always a toss-up whether they're going to ask me for my autograph or smack me in the mouth."

George Best

"You can't beat Sinatra. I was actually supposed to have dinner with him one night, but we lost to Charlton so I cancelled it and went home!"

Sir Alex Ferguson

THE MEN IN BLACK

"Everyone knows that for us to get awarded a penalty we need a certificate from the Pope and a personal letter from the Queen."

Sir Alex Ferguson after Leeds were awarded a spot kick

"If he fouls you he normally picks you up, but the referee doesn't see what he picks you up by."

Ryan Giggs on Dennis Wise

"People say we've got the best referees in the world. I shudder to think what the rest are like."

Martin Buchan

"It must be necessary for a player to bring a gun and shoot one of our men in the box for us to get a penalty."

Assistant manager Carlos Queiroz fumes after Cristiano Ronaldo's penalty appeal is turned away

"It was the 95th minute of their usual seven minutes of injury time."

Sir Alex Ferguson

"In the tunnel, I say to David Elleray, 'You might as well book me now and get it over with'. He takes it pretty well but he still books me."

Roy Keane

"The pace of the game demanded a referee who was fit. It is an indictment of our game. You see referees abroad who are as fit as butcher's dogs. We have some who are fit. He wasn't fit. He was taking 30 seconds to book a player. He was needing a rest. It was ridiculous."

Sir Alex Ferguson on referee Alan Wiley

"Some referees don't like it. They don't like the truth. But I just told him how bad he was in the first-half."

Sir Alex Ferguson on referee Mark Clattenburg

"They were like a pack of wolves. I've never seen so much hatred on players' faces. It looked as though they were trying to put pressure on Andy D'Urso so that he wouldn't send off Jaap Stam as well as giving the penalty decision."

Keith Cooper, referees assessor and former referee

"I think if the referee had stood still, we wouldn't have chased him."

Roy Keane on Andy D'Urso

"Sir Alex Ferguson once complimented me on my handling of a game. Three weeks later, after I'd refereed another United match, he pulled me aside and said, 'Well Jeff, back to normal. F*cking business as usual'."

Referee Jeff Winter

"I don't know about making referees professional. They love themselves enough as it is now."

Paul Scholes

"Dennis Wise could start a fight in an empty house."

Sir Alex Ferguson

"He's grinning. 'You pr*ck'. He gestures dismissively. The red card comes out. Shearer's right. I am a pr*ck."

Roy Keane on an altercation with Alan Shearer

"I have just been unlucky."

Paul Scholes on his 90 yellow and four red cards

"Can anyone tell me why they give referees a watch? It certainly isn't to keep the time."

Sir Alex Ferguson

"Cristiano. Why would he want to go down? He was on a hat-trick, he had gone round the keeper and was brought down. It was a ridiculous decision."

Sir Alex Ferguson

EGO MANIAC

"I don't need to demonstrate that I am the no.1 in the world. If I am named the best in the world, it won't be a surprise to me."

Cristiano Ronaldo

"Pele said he thought I was the greatest ever player. I have always thought I was the best ever player – that's the way you have to look at it. I have never looked at another player and felt inferior."

George Best

"It's bloody tough being a legend."

Ron Atkinson

"I am very arrogant. I am one of the best managers of the world."

Louis van Gaal

"I'm better than Pele. I can kick with both feet."

George Best

"I don't need to say, 'I'm in the history of football, I'm a legend'. The numbers say everything."

Cristiano Ronaldo

"I met Mick Jagger when I played for Oxford United and the Rolling Stones did a show there. Little did I know he'd be as famous as me one day."

Ron Atkinson

"It's true lots of people hate me but there are even more who love me and who support me. I feel bad only when I play badly. Fortunately that happens rarely."

Cristiano Ronaldo

"I can play in the 11 positions because a good player can play anywhere."

Zlatan Ibrahimovic

"I will be beautiful again in four or five days."

Cristiano Ronaldo reassures his admirers

after being elbowed in face

"If people want to call me the saviour of

Manchester United, that's not a problem

for me."

Ruud van Nistelrooy

"I sometimes think I must be the only person

in Britain who has featured on the front, centre

and back pages of a daily newspaper – all on

the same day."

George Best

"People whistle me because I am good looking, rich and a great footballer. They are jealous of me."

Cristiano Ronaldo

"I don't do anything... nothing! I delegate. I delegate and I earn a lot of money."

Louis van Gaal

"Over the years a lot of great players have left United – I'm sure the same will happen to me one day."

Roy Keane

"It is the best I have scored. It was a fantastic strike and I can't wait to see it again on DVD."
Cristiano Ronaldo after scoring a 40-yard goal against Porto

"I don't really class myself as a footballer. I call myself an entertainer."
George Best

"I won't be King of Manchester. I will be God of Manchester."
Zlatan Ibrahimovic

"I am the first, second and third best player in the world."

Cristiano Ronaldo

"Absolutely not. I have ordered a plane. It is much faster."

Zlatan Ibrahimovic on rumours he bought a Porsche

"If I'd been born ugly, you'd never have heard of Pele."

George Best

"Is Rooney as good as me? Don't be silly!"

George Best

"I think I deserve to win!"

Cristiano Ronaldo on being nominated for PFA Footballer of the Year – and he ended up winning it

"I am such a bloody talented guy. I might go into painting or something like that."

Sir Alex Ferguson

"I always had the belief that if you put five men in front of me, I could go past them all."

Cristiano Ronaldo

SAY THAT AGAIN?

"Peaks of happiness and depths of pain – just like the chain of mountains in the Alps where I am going to rest and paint."

Eric Cantona

"My parents have been there for me, ever since I was about seven."

David Beckham

"I came home and said to my dad, 'Are we Irish?' He replied: 'How do I know?'"

Wayne Rooney

Say That Again?

"We're at the top of the cliff and we can either fall off the edge or keep climbing."
Gary Neville

"When an Italian tells me it's pasta on the plate I check under the sauce to make sure. They're the inventors of the smokescreen."
Sir Alex Ferguson

"I've got a contract with United until 2010, but my future belongs to God."
Cristiano Ronaldo

"I feel I can still do the same job as I did 10 years ago – I've just got a few more wrinkles."

David Beckham

"If, as some people think, there is such a thing as reincarnation, I'd love to come back as an eagle. I love the way eagles move, the way they soar, the way they gaze."

Eric Cantona

"If Chelsea drop points, the cat's out in the open. And you know what cats are like – sometimes they don't come home."

Sir Alex Ferguson

Say That Again?

"I was really surprised when the FA knocked on my doorbell."

Michael Owen

"Apparently when you head a football, you lose brain cells, but it doesn't bother me... I'm a horse. No one's proved it yet have they?"

David May

"Going to sleep guys gonna count 19 sheep to help me sleep.
#whenwasurlastleaguewasibornohyeahbarley"

Wayne Rooney not getting the gist of Twitter's hashtags

"You can play chess for about 10 hours and still lose, know what I mean?"

Sir Alex Ferguson

"It is pretty nerve-racking but I've enjoyed the whole night. I've got a little bit of a headache, that's how nerve-racking it was, but I've enjoyed the whole night."

David Beckham speaking after the Sports Personality of the Year show

"It will be a difficult couple of days. It's difficult now and it will be difficult tomorrow."

Gary Neville

Say That Again?

"The unthinkable is not something we are thinking about at the moment."
United chief executive Peter Kenyon

"I might have said that, but on the whole I talk a lot of rubbish."
Eric Cantona

"@WayneRooney I'll put u asleep within 10 seconds u little girl. Don't say stuff and not follow up on it. I'll be waiting"
Wayne Rooney picking a Twitter fight with himself

"The problem is not what we are doing badly, it is because we are not doing things well."

Patrice Evra

"Thank you for letting me play in your beautiful football."

Eric Cantona after winning the 1994 PFA Player of the Year award

"We have made it an uphill task for ourselves – a very uphill task."

David Beckham on United's disappointing run of form

"A survey was conducted of the world's female population asking them if they would sleep with Bill Clinton. 80 per cent of them answered, 'What again?'"

Peter Schmeichel tells a gag

"You shouldn't be nuts, but it doesn't matter if you are a bit peculiar."

Peter Schmeichel

"Maths is totally done differently to what I was teached when I was at school."

David Beckham. And English too?

"It's not just the manager who makes the decision, it's the player who makes the decision. They both decide fifty-fifty to make a decision."

Ruud van Nistelrooy

"I definitely want Brooklyn to be christened, but I don't know into what religion yet."

David Beckham

"When he waggled his hips he made the stanchions in the grandstand sway."

Harry Gregg on Eddie Colman

Say That Again?

"In football you have adversary; in cinema that adversary is yourself."

Eric Cantona

"Wazza is in the groove. He is a spurter."

Rio Ferdinand on Wayne Rooney

"There's no one to blame – they're just individual mistakes."

David Beckham

"I no speak England very good mate."

Anderson

"It's when Paul Scholes isn't playing that Manchester United miss him."

Former United star Arthur Albiston

"Gary Neville was captain and now Ryan Giggs has taken on the mantelpiece."

Rio Ferdinand

"That was in the past – we're in the future now."

David Beckham

"It's a conflict of parallels."

Sir Alex Ferguson

Say That Again?

"I will never find any difference between Pele's pass to Carlos Alberto in the final of the 1970 World Cup and the poetry of young Rimbaud."

Eric Cantona

"As with every young player he's only 18."

Sir Alex Ferguson

"He was a quiet man, Eric Cantona, but he was a man of few words."

David Beckham

"Mr bean. Funny"

Wayne Rooney tweets his film review

"Alex Ferguson is the best manager I've ever had at this level. Well, he's the only manager I've actually had at this level. But he's the best manager I've ever had."

David Beckham

"Confidence seems to be draining away. You can invisibly see that."

Michael Owen

"It was a draw, so in the end we didn't win."

David Beckham after United are held by Croatia Zagreb

Say That Again?

"Hi rio do u want picking up in the morning pal"

Wayne Rooney's first tweet was the best

"It's different – it's not the same."

Ryan Giggs

"A goal-scorer has always scored goals."

David Moyes

"When the seagulls follow the trawler, it's because they think sardines will be thrown into the sea. Thank you very much."

Eric Cantona

"So I don't think there is a lot of distance between Tottenham and Manchester United, but the distance is in points. They have won more, they are scoring more and that's because they have more creative players."

Louis van Gaal says there isn't much between Tottenham and United, apart from the major fact Spurs score more goals

"Often there are players who have only football as a way of expressing themselves and never develop other interests. And when they no longer play football, they no longer do anything; they no longer exist, or rather they have the sensation of no longer existing."

Eric Cantona

Say That Again?

"If you win things you get the white stuff, but if you don't win things, you get all the black stuff."
Peter Schmeichel on the media's coverage of Sir Alex Ferguson

"I'm not that bloke Mystic Meg."
Rio Ferdinand gets the sex of his astrologers confused

"What we have to do is put our teeth into the Premiership."
Peter Schmeichel

"I'm going to tell you the story about the geese which fly 5,000 miles from Canada to France. They fly in V-formation but the second ones don't fly. They're the subs for the first ones. And then the second ones take over – so it's teamwork."

Sir Alex Ferguson

Printed in Great Britain
by Amazon